An Astronaut's LIFE

Pebble® Plus

Becoming an ASTRONAUT

by Martha E. H. Rustad

CAPSTONE PRESS
a capstone imprint

Pebble Plus is published by Capstone Press,
1710 Roe Crest Drive, North Mankato, Minnesota 56003
www.mycapstone.com

Library of Congress Cataloging-in-Publication Data is available on the Library of Congress website.
ISBN 978-1-5157-9819-4 (library binding)
ISBN 978-1-5157-9823-1 (paperback)
ISBN 978-1-5157-9827-9 (eBook PDF)

Editorial Credits

Abby Colich, editor; Kyle Grenz, designer; Tracy Cummins, media researcher;
Kathy McColley, production specialist

Photo Credits

NASA Image and Video Library: Cover, 11, 13, 15, 17, 19; Shutterstock: Alexey Y. Petrov, 9,
Aphelleon, Design Element, d1sk, Design Element, Back Cover, Lone Pine, 21, muratart, 5, science
photo, 7, Zakharchuk, Design Element

Note to Parents and Teachers

The An Astronaut's Life set supports science standards related to space. This book describes and
illustrates how people become astronauts. The images support early readers in understanding
the text. The repetition of words and phrases helps early readers learn new words. This book also
introduces early readers to subject-specific vocabulary words, which are defined in the Glossary
section. Early readers may need assistance to read some words and to use the Table of Contents,
Glossary, Read More, Internet Sites, Critical Thinking Questions, and Index sections of the book.

Printed and bound in the USA.
010768S18

Table of Contents

How to Be an Astronaut 4

Astronaut Training. 12

Going to Space! 20

Glossary. 22
Read More 23
Internet Sites 23
Critical Thinking Questions 24
Index 24

How to Be an Astronaut

You look out a window.
It is dark. You see a
big blue circle. It is
planet Earth. Do you dream
of going to space?

The path to being an astronaut starts early. People who want to be astronauts study science. They study math too. They go to school for many years.

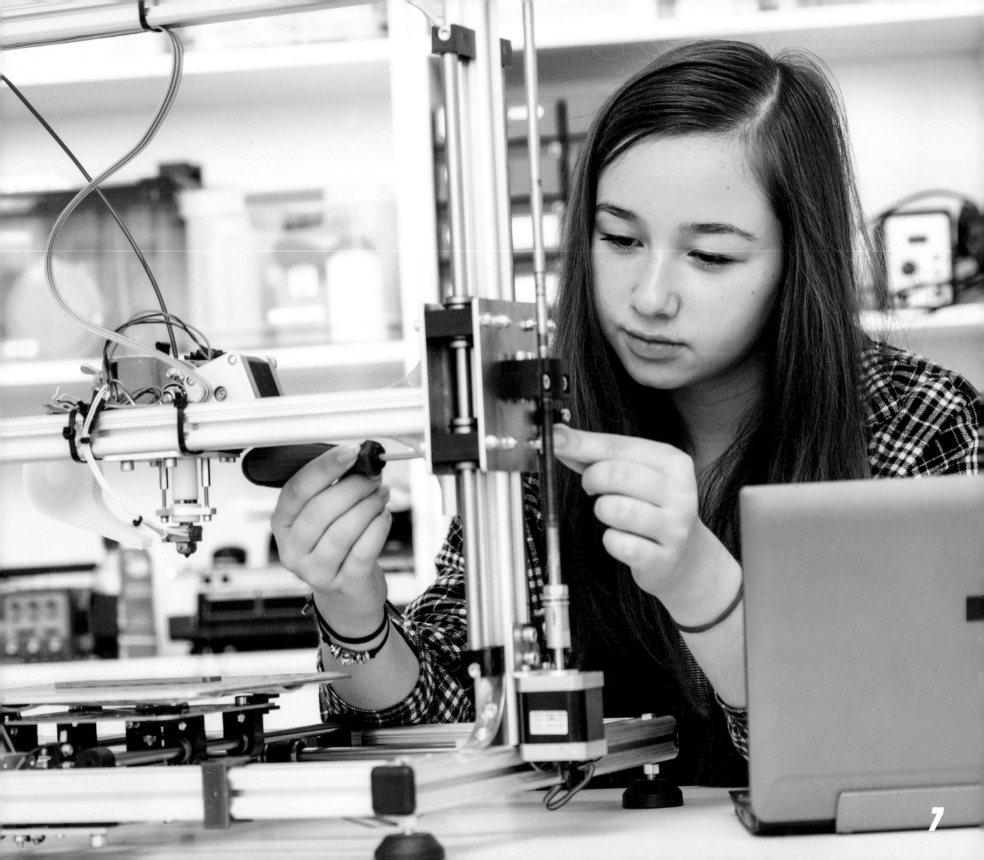

Astronauts must work another job first.

Many become pilots. They learn

how to fly jets. They fly

for 1,000 hours or more.

Many people want to be astronauts.

Only a few are chosen to train.

Good health and eyesight are needed.

Size matters too. Astronauts must fit

in space suits and the spacecraft.

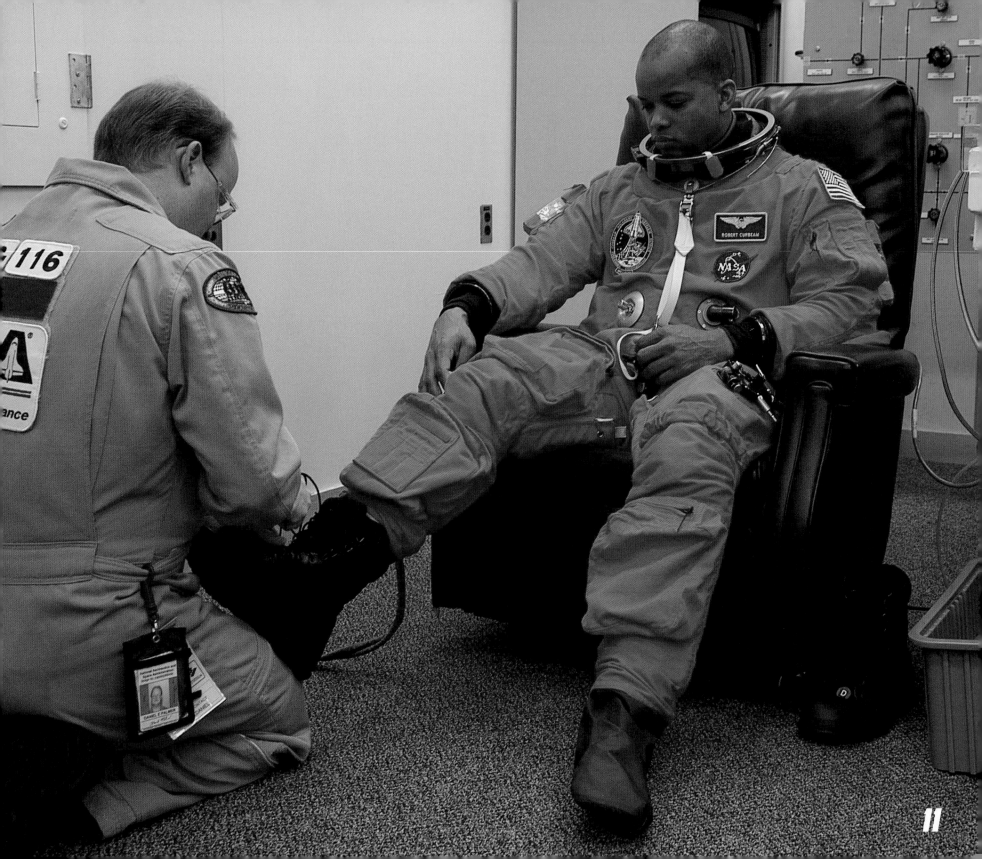

Astronaut Training

Training lasts for two years
or more. Astronauts learn how
to fly spacecraft. They work
in rooms that look like the inside of
spacecraft. They practice using robots.

Astronauts learn how to do their jobs in space. Some will be pilots. Others will lead missions. Some will care for cargo. Others will do experiments.

Being underwater feels a little like space does. Astronauts must know how to swim. They train in a pool. They use scuba gear. They wear space suits in the water.

Training flights help astronauts
get ready for space. A jet flies
very high. People feel weightless.
They may get sick. They call
the jet the "vomit comet."

Going to Space!

Finally, it's time to go
to space. The astronauts know
what to do. Get ready
to count down.
Three. Two. One. Blastoff!

GLOSSARY

cargo (KAHR-goh)—the goods carried by a ship, vehicle, or aircraft

experiment (ik-SPEER-uh-muhnt)—a test to find out if something works

mission (MISH-uhn)—a planned job or task

scuba (SCOO-bah)—equipment that lets people breathe underwater

spacecraft (SPAYSS-kraft)—a vehicle that travels in space

weightless (WATE-less)—a feeling of floating; people feel weightless in space because there is no gravity to pull them down

vomit (VOM-it)—to throw up food and liquid from your stomach through your mouth

READ MORE

Clay, Kathryn. *Astronaut in Training.* Smithsonian Little Explorer: Little Astronauts. North Mankato, Minn.: Capstone, 2017.

Jones, Tom. *Ask the Astronaut: A Galaxy of Astonishing Answers to Your Questions on Spaceflight.* Washington, D.C.: Smithsonian Books, 2016.

West, David. *Lots of Things You Want to Know about Astronauts: . . . And Some You Don't!* Mankato, Minn.: Smart Apple Media, 2016.

INTERNET SITES

Use FactHound to find Internet sites related to this book.

Visit *www.facthound.com*

Just type in 9781515798194 and go.

Check out projects, games and lots more at
www.capstonekids.com

CRITICAL THINKING QUESTIONS

1. Name one way astronauts train before going into space.

2. Look at the photos on pages 17 and 19. Then reread the text on the opposite pages. Where are the astronauts in each photo?

3. Astronauts train for a long time before going to space. What do you think would happen if they did not train or trained for only a short time? Explain your answer.

INDEX

Earth, 4

health, 10

jobs, 8, 14

pilots, 8, 14

robots, 12

school, 6
spacecraft, 10, 12
space suits, 10, 16